ADVENTURES OF MEWMEW THE FERAL CAT

A TRUE STORY

by

Luba Bradwell

Recommended for the 8-13 age group.
Interesting and funny reading for parents too!

ACKNOWLEDGMENTS

Many thanks to Sarah Pekich, my good friend, and a talented photographer, for her assistance with, and critique of, my photographs, helpful suggestions, and confidence in my ability to compile this book.

Thanks also to Lori Anglin, President of Metro Ferals, an organization promoting trap, neuter and return to their former outdoor abode, of feral cats in the metro communities of Washington, D.C. (including the suburbs of Maryland and Virginia, and as far away as Baltimore and points beyond), and especially for her assistance in trapping, transporting, arranging for neutering and treatment of MewMew the feral cat whose adventures are depicted in this book.

Also a warm thank you to Alley Cat Allies, a national organization dedicated to the welfare and care of feral cats under their banner of "trap, neuter and return to their former abode" (TNR), for the inspiration and invaluable information about feral cats in general provided to the writer of this book.

This book could not have been written without the help and affection of my son, Aaron, for the cat.

CONTENTS

INTRODUCTION: WHAT IS A FERAL CAT?

A feral (wild) cat is not another word for stray. A stray is a cat who was abandoned or just got lost. Stray cats can usually be adopted. Adult feral cats are wild cats and cannot be adopted. Maybe you've seen them behind a restaurant, in an alley or in a park. They have never had a real home and unless a caretaker provided food for an outdoor feral, they are usually left to fend for themselves, looking for scraps of food or a bit of shelter. Feral cats are afraid of people since they grew up without human contact; therefore, they do not make good pets and cannot adjust to living indoors with a human family. It is important to understand that these wild cats are similar to raccoons, possums, or any other untamed, outdoor animal. Some feral cats live in family groups called "colonies;" some feral cats are descended from rural barn cats.

Feral cats can live almost anywhere and they live all over the world. Feral kittens, on the other hand, if captured early and socialized with a family, can be placed for adoption. Feral cats eat rodents, small mammals, and insects, but they also like to eat people food out of the garbage. A lot of people feed feral cats, not just in the United States, but almost everywhere. Italians take pride in feeding the famous black cats of Venice, and in Asia, Buddhist monks feed cats. Ancient Egyptians worshipped cats as creatures sent by Gods who bring people luck.

1

People feed feral cats because they are kind-hearted and don't want to see cats go hungry. They also feed them because they enjoy watching these beautiful animals and because they enjoy their company. Feral cats develop a relationship with the people who feed them and often run out to greet their feeders. Most feral cats are happy, especially if someone is giving them good food every day. However, nature can be cruel, and many feral kittens die of kittenhood diseases. To make up for the kittens that die, cats have lots and lots of kittens, which can be very hard on the mother cats.

Often the people who care about feral cats will catch them and take them to a vet. The vet will sterilize the cats so that they won't have more kittens, and then vaccinate them against diseases and treat any illness or injury that the cat has. Once the cats are sterilized their lives become much easier. The female cats no longer have kittens constantly, so they can eat and rest, and, since no kittens are born, no kittens suffer and die. The male cats stop fighting over female cats. In addition to these benefits, it has been said that sterilization protects the cats from cancer and several other "diseases."

Another thing that kind people do for feral cats is build or buy them shelters to protect them from the weather. In parts of the country where it gets cold, these shelters are insulated and keep the cats nice and warm. However, if feral cats are not given shelter by kind people, they often find other shelters. Some cats find warm places under porches, or in the crawlspaces of buildings; other cats may go underground, into drainage pipes or sewer tunnels. Although these places are not as nice as the shelters people build for cats, they do help the cats survive harsh weather. When the cats are fed, protected from weather, sterilized, and vaccinated, they are very happy and may lead long, healthy lives.

Alley Cat Allies is an organization that advocates the "trap, neuter and return" policy (TNR). This means that one can obtain traps from their community organizations such as the Humane Society, or other places (see alleycat.org on the web for additional information). This organization also provides information on where to find discounted spay/neuter and veterinary services.

After treatment, the cats are returned to their original neighborhood, hopefully to live out their days as healthy and happy cats. TNR works and is a proven procedure in which entire colonies of stray and feral cats are humanely trapped, then evaluated, vaccinated, and neutered by veterinarians. Most kittens and tame cats are adopted into good homes. Adult cats that are too wild to be adopted are returned to live out their lives under the watchful care of sympathetic neighborhood volunteers in their previous surroundings. The breeding stops, and cat populations are gradually reduced. Nuisance behaviors associated with breeding, such as the yowling of females or the spraying of tom cats are virtually eliminated.

Disease and malnutrition are greatly reduced. Ongoing care creates a safety net for the cats and the community.

[Reprinted with permission from Alley Cat Allies, an organization formed to promote the education and general welfare of feral cats everywhere.]

OUT OF THE SHADOW

Out of the shadow and seemingly from nowhere, a large black tom cat, somewhat straggly looking, a little thin and bedraggled, appeared in front of my townhouse in suburban Fairfax County, Virginia. He mewed in a soft sweet way that caught my immediate attention, and as I sat on my front entrance stoop, I called out to him "Kitty, kitty!" He continued his soft mewing while I looked at him and tried to approach to pet him. He dashed quickly away from my presence, as if anticipating harm. As I had not had previous encounters with feral cats, I did not understand that they were shy, skittish, and afraid of human contact.

I went into the house and brought out a can of wet food (I also have two "house-and-yard" cats). I stirred the food and heaped it in a pile for easier consumption. The cat moved quickly forward, all the time looking at me to make sure that I would not interfere. He devoured the food while looking around every few seconds to see if someone was coming, and continued his mewing while doing so. Thus I named him MewMew. After finishing his meal he rolled over on his back and lifted his paws, taking care that he would not be touched. He had many sweet and endearing ways about him. In the coming days, he was so anxious to eat that he would try to knock his food out of my hands before I had a chance to place it down on my front stoop, and on occasion it would spill onto the concrete. This did not deter him from trying to knock the food out of my hands again during the next feeding cycle, and then devouring every morsel, rain or shine. As days went by, however, he continued running away as I tried to reach out and pet him.

From the first day of our encounter, MewMew stopped by the house at approximately the same time almost every day. Upon seeing him on my front stoop, I put out his food. He was always hungry, and as soon as he was through eating, he would mew pitifully as if asking for more. I realized that perhaps feeding him once a day was not enough, and I began putting something out for him in the early evening, as well as in the morning. I would call out "Kitty, kitty!" on the days that he was not on the stoop, and he would come running from out of the bushes across the alley. I could see him through my glass door, sticking his face against the glass, anxiously awaiting arrival of the food. On occasion I would attempt to pet him while he ate. He jerked his body as if from a shock. Over time he seemed to relax somewhat at my attention, and he ultimately permitted me to pet him, but only briefly, and only on his back. When I tried to pet him while he was rolled over, he tried to nip at me with his claws. MewMew was a shrewd creature, always keeping me at an arm's length while at the same time allowing me a tiny measure of his affection.

MewMew finally gained weight and filled out nicely. He became a handsome, large tom cat, with dark red highlights appearing as the sun shone on his thick black coat. I often wondered where he roamed when I did not see him.

Thus began a relationship that was sometimes funny and at other times sad. Days turned into weeks and months, and beautiful spring and summer weather was giving way to cold winds and lots of rain. While I was concerned that MewMew needed shelter from the cold, I noticed that he did not seem to mind the wind and the rain, coming around and eating as usual on a daily basis. He must have found a place where he was sheltered from the weather, or maybe because he was used to being out in the weather, he did not seem to be much affected by it. My son Aaron mentioned that he thought he saw him across the street from our house the previous winter, before we ever knew him, but MewMew never came around to our house until this year.

During the snow storm, when MewMew appeared, I cleared an area on the front stoop with a shovel and laid a thick pad of newspapers so that he would not have to stand on icy concrete. MewMew stood on that pile and ate his food, even though the soft snowflakes covered his shiny black coat until he was soaking wet.

I went to a pet store to look for a shelter that might be suitable for MewMew. I was shown a plastic igloo. It had a very small entry opening, and was unsightly. The igloo was as cold inside as the weather was outside, as it was not insulated. I was certain that MewMew would never enter one of those, and even if he did, he would not find comfort therein. I called Best Friends Animal Society of Utah, the largest animal sanctuary in America, to which I made contributions, and spoke to a person there who was knowledgeable about feral cats. I was informed that Styrofoam containers made good shelters, since they were insulated from heat and cold, and if a couple of containers could be glued together, they would provide a shelter which would be large enough to house MewMew. The lady at the sanctuary mailed me a leaflet, containing instructions on how to assemble a shelter out of Styrofoam.

My son-in-law made a wonderful Styrofoam shelter from two boxes, complete with an awning, to keep out the elements. We lined it with straw to absorb the moisture and make the floor soft and pleasant to sit on. When I stuck my arm inside this container, it actually felt to be of comfortable temperature. We reinforced it with a couple of bricks on top of the roof so that during high winds it would not blow away. The shelter was placed by the fence next to our outdoor front stoop, only a few feet from where MewMew ate. Unfortunately, MewMew was oblivious to the benefits of this construction, and would not even go near it all winter long. We tried everything, including placing his food at the entrance to the shelter. We reasoned that perhaps MewMew was weary of traps because of a previous experience, or was just somehow spooked by any enclosure, but for whatever reason, he refused to go into this shelter, so there was nothing else that we could do to provide him protection from the weather.

LOOKING FOR SERVICES

I realized that MewMew needed to be vaccinated for rabies, and I also wanted to have him neutered. However, there was the problem of catching him, so I called a few veterinary offices to find out if there was a way to trap him, a facility that I could take him to, and the approximate cost of doing so. I was looking for an inexpensive facility. After all, I felt that if I was caring for a wild cat, at the very least I would expect some help from the Humane Society, a feral cat association or a similar agency, to help with costs to take care of his many initial needs.

I ultimately heard that there was a local organization serving the feral cats in my area, called Metro Ferals, and I called them to find out what to do. I was told to come by and pick up a trap to humanely capture MewMew, and I would be shown how to use it. If and when I was able to trap and transport MewMew back to Metro Ferals, they would take him to a veterinary clinic that they normally frequented in the city, have him neutered, and provide him with shots and a general check-up, all at a very nominal cost to me. Then he would be returned in the cat carrier that I provided, and released to the same location where he had been captured, to hopefully live out his days as a healthy and happy cat. Needless to say, I was elated by this information.

After several attempts at setting up the trap, Aaron called Metro Ferals and found out how to do it. He then successfully set the trap. We placed some tuna inside as bait, and lined the bottom with newspaper for sitting comfort.

Unfortunately, as with our cat weather shelter, MewMew refused to enter the trap. I was becoming exasperated, not knowing what else I could do to capture him. I was advised to withhold food from MewMew for as long as five days, if need be. I did not want to do this, however, because I considered it to be cruel. Besides, I figured that even if I did not provide food, MewMew would find a way to survive, as he did before we ever knew him. I reasoned that withholding food for that long might cause MewMew to just disappear, and the whole exercise would have served no purpose except to keep the cat hungry for a long time. I did, however, withhold the food for one day before trying to trap him, but this did not help either. As time went on, I kept trying again and again, but MewMew would not enter the trap. Periodically, I would call Lori at Metro Ferals and complain that I was not able to trap MewMew. I even offered to pay someone for trapping the cat, and Lori said she would look into this and see what she could do. However, she was not able to locate anyone to do this, and the next time I called her, she indicated that since I was not successful at using the trap, to please return it, as she needed it back. I did this with a heavy heart.

DISAPPEARANCE OF MEWMEW

One morning, as was customary, I went out to my entry stoop with MewMew's food on a sheet of foil and a can of fresh water, but MewMew was nowhere to be seen. I called his name and "kitty, kitty" several times, to no avail. By now I was very attached to this cat. I went around the neighborhood looking to see if perhaps he was injured and hiding behind some bush, calling his name as I went around. I considered posting signs or flyers in the neighborhood, but decided against it since this was a feral who did not have a tag or a collar, and thus was not readily identifiable; and, being a wild cat, he would be very difficult, if not impossible, to catch.

As the hours passed my concern grew, and I became very nervous and agitated. I could not eat my lunch, and as suppertime approached, I went out looking again, hoping that since MewMew did not eat that morning, he may be hungry and thus appear for supper. MewMew did not appear that evening nor that night, nor the next morning. As days went on without MewMew, an unhappy and bone-chilling thought was creeping into my mind that maybe I would never see the cat again, the cat that I cared for, fed, and lovingly looked after for so many months.

I called our local animal shelter and was advised that no cat was delivered to that facility matching the description that I provided. I called our Humane Society and spoke to their volunteer who tried to allay my fears.

I was advised to just be patient, that at times cats disappeared and roamed or were even fed by others, but that eventually they may reappear. Having spoken to the Society's volunteer, I felt better and was able to compose my jitters, and prepared myself for a long wait.

As days went by, my hopes of ever seeing MewMew were diminishing, and a feeling of sadness and helplessness enveloped me.

I couldn't help remembering the sad story told by my friend whose two kittens I adopted. A story of my cat Tiss's father, a large handsome black tom cat, named Warlock, who disappeared on Halloween day. One minute Warlock was sitting on the hood of the car, and a few minutes later, just before being called in prior to sunset and the ensuing Halloween celebrations, he disappeared, never to be seen again. Since hearing that sad story, I decided to never let my cats out on Halloween day. Unfortunately, I would not be able to control a similar situation involving a feral cat, whose permanent home is in the alley. Remembering that sad story made me feel even worse.

In the early evening of the fourth day of MewMew's disappearance, as I sat on the steps of my front stoop, I heard a faint mewing coming from the bushes across the alley where MewMew often visited. I ran inside the house and called my son, Aaron, to come out and listen to see if he could identify the mewing, that I did not recognize as being that of our MewMew. Aaron came out and said he thought that it was MewMew. I quickly went into the kitchen and prepared some food. I called to MewMew but he would not come out of the bushes. I left the food on the stoop as usual, closed the door and waited.

After a short time MewMew appeared, although acting somewhat skittish, and started to eat. Aaron went out to look at him and came back noting that something happened to MewMew, that his fur was badly matted and bloody on one side of his face and neck. At that particular time I did not realize the seriousness of MewMew's injuries. I was so happy to see him back.

Later I was able to take a closer look at the cat and realized that he must have gotten into a serious fight with either another cat, a dog, a raccoon, or a possum. I was not sure which, as all of those animals wandered around our neighborhood, and I knew it must have been one of them. It was probably not a dog, since all the dogs I ever see are being walked on a leash, and the County has a very strict leash law. The injury needed to be quickly treated, for an infection could set in at any time and thus result in serious illness or even death. The urgency of treatment and the need for a rabies shot were apparent. This situation was becoming critical, and was consuming my thoughts with each passing day. I called Lori of Metro Ferals asking if I could pick up the trap once again, and explained to her what had happened to MewMew.

I picked up and set the trap and went on with the business of capturing the cat. I prayed at night promising God that I would get down on my knees and thank Him every day of my life (as long as I was able to do so), if He would only let me trap MewMew so that the cat could be treated for his injuries and receive other services which he so desperately needed.

The next day I re-set the trap by placing tuna into it as I had previously, and lined the bottom with newspapers for seating comfort. I called MewMew and he came. He did not look well. As he stood in front of me, I dragged my finger around the trap as if drawing a form around it. MewMew followed my finger right into the trap, growling softly, and I pushed the trap's door shut even as MewMew was inside but somehow the door was still open. My heart skipped a beat. I could not believe that finally, after so many tries, my efforts paid off. I was so exhilarated that I literally jumped for joy. Upon further thought, I realized that it was due to the Lord's divine intervention that I was able to capture MewMew, for I believed in the power of prayer, and that because of it, the trapping and ensuing services for the poor cat were finally at hand. MewMew was mewing loudly as if protesting this inhumane occurrence. I felt sorry for him, but at the same time I was sure that he would eventually realize that this fleeting discomfort would ultimately save his life.

MEWMEW RECEIVES THE NEEDED SERVICES

I called Lori and told her that I was on the way with MewMew, for her to take the cat to the vet as she advised that she would do. Lori said she would start the cat on antibiotic treatment immediately, and would take him to the vet the next morning. Since my car was not functional at the time, I had a friend to help me transport MewMew to Metro Ferals, a trip of about 45 minutes by car.

When we arrived, Lori took me to her back yard where a large structure resembling a barn was built to house feral cats needing special care, or just temporarily housed there for future placement. There were cats of every shape, color and size in the house. Some were climbing up on rafters and shelves close to the ceiling, which were built expressly for that purpose. There were other shelves and enclosures built to accommodate cats who wished to hide, or to find a secluded corner in which to rest. I was especially taken with two beautiful cats – one huge long-haired black and one gorgeous gray cat, both of whom did not object to being petted. In fact they appeared to be quite tame. There was also a gigantic older orange cat, that elicited attention, and was easy to pet. There were small kittens and nursing kittens there too. There was a blind cat, a feline leukemia cat (who could live for a long time if kept in a place where she would not be injured or exposed to other diseases), and a small kitty who was born with an injured back leg that had been amputated, but seemed to be doing well. There were many wild cats who would not accept human contact, but there were also some cats who wished to be petted. There was even a cat who, I was told, liked to be vacuumed (possibly he thought he was receiving a massage). I was completely taken with this incredible gathering of so many different cats, in a house which was devoid of bad smells, and which appeared to be clean, tidy and well kept. There were large and small cages there too, for cats who were nursing or who needed to be isolated for short times.

Lori advised that some of the cats were waiting to be sent to horse farms where rodents presented problems with horse feed, and the feral cats could correct this condition. Other cats, such as kittens who could be socialized and become used to humans, would be placed for adoption. Lori noted that kittens slated for adoption to good homes, would be spayed or neutered, and receive all the shots beforehand; therefore, the fee charged for adoption would include these services, and the overage used to care for, and feed the remaining cats. At that particular time there were approximately 60 cats in that house. I remember Lori saying she used 36 cans of cat food to feed them daily!

When I got home I could not stop thinking about that feral house and what a wonder it was. How amazing it was to realize the dedication and love that some people possessed for the poor homeless cats.

A house built specially for feral cats by Lori Anglin, President of Metro Ferals, where 60 feral cats who needed special attention, or were awaiting placement, now live in climate-controlled comfort.

Lori called late the following day and told me that MewMew needed 21 stitches to close the wounds on his face and neck. All other services, such as neutering, shots, deworming, flea treatment, ear cleaning, etc., had also been done. Lori said that the stitches were metal, and therefore would have to be removed in two weeks. She would keep the cat in a separate large cage in her cat house to prevent any run-in with the other cats, and to give the stitches a better chance to heal. Two days later Lori called saying that MewMew was restless and was not doing too well, and that he made a big mess turning over his litter box.

Not having been accustomed to a living environment with so many cats, MewMew may have thought that because of misbehaving, he was being punished, by being put through his worst nightmare. Even more frightening, he may have thought he had advanced to his ninth (and last) life, by descending into a house of horrors, surrounded by 60 strange cats.

Lori asked if I had a place in my house to keep MewMew for the next twelve days, where he could be isolated and safe before the stitches could be removed. I told Lori that my basement utility room was quite large and that I thought MewMew would be well placed therein.

The next day Lori arrived at my house accompanied by the vet technician, carrying MewMew in the large cat carrier that I previously provided for his eventual return. The two ladies looked around my utility room and noted the fact that there were rafters under the ceiling and that the cat could possibly hide there, but otherwise they decided that the place was clean, safe, large enough, and isolated from the rest of the house, so as not to needlessly stress the cat. So started one of the most frightening experiences of my life.

ADVENTURES IN THE RAFTERS

The first few days went well. MewMew was initially shy and skittish, as unfamiliar surroundings would cause him to be. He ran and hid every time the door to the utility room opened (of course we kept it closed at all times so the cat could not come into the house and have a run-in with my two cats). Most of the time MewMew spent hiding behind the washer-dryer by the corner wall, or he was hiding behind a storage door and other equipment on the other side of the room. When the litter box was cleaned, as it was daily, or the food came twice a day as usual, MewMew would run up to me and let me pet him. He devoured his food as he always did, then ran and hid. He used the litter box faithfully. Things could not have been going better.

The stitches looked to be healing nicely as I continued to daily place the antibiotic medication in his food, as directed by the vet. The day was fast approaching when the stitches would come out, thus freeing the cat to be put outdoors to take up his usual lifestyle of rolling in the grass, running after the squirrels and the leaves, sitting among the flowering trees and the lush lawns of common areas in the back of the townhouses, especially since it was spring and the weather would soon be warm, or trying to catch up with my two house-and-yard cats, which he never could, because he wasn't nearly as fast nor as agile as those two. Unfortunately, neither of my cats would have anything to do with MewMew, nor did they like him. In

19

fact they didn't even like each other. My smallish tabby, Toots, although now five years old, was about half the size of MewMew, and I felt that she was a bit afraid and intimidated by him. She would look around every time the door was opened for her to go out. When she did not see MewMew she would dash out and run, and if he suddenly appeared, she would run to, and jump on top of, the patio fence. She could actually leap onto the fence as well as, if not better than, any squirrel. All MewMew seemed to be able to do then was to sit below and look up at her. My other cat was also a black cat, but of average size. Tiss seemed to hold her own around MewMew, however, even she would hiss every time MewMew came too close or when they were facing each other.

The time, when the 21 stitches needed to close the wounds of MewMew's face and neck were to come out, was fast approaching. When that day came, I telephoned Lori, and she advised that she and the vet technician would be arriving around noon of the following day to sedate MewMew and remove the stitches at my house. I thought that we would still keep MewMew indoors for a day or two after the stitches were out, to allow the skin to settle in the warmer indoor climate. Even though it was now spring and it should have been warm, some days were still quite cool.

On the fateful day that Lori and the vet technician were to arrive, I fed MewMew as usual. In fact, before they arrived, I saw him come out from behind the washer-dryer. He lingered for a while and let me pet him as he had been doing for some time now. The cat carrier which was supposed to hold him in order to apply the mild sedative before the stitches were to be removed was ready, hidden from sight outside the utility room door. The plan was to grab MewMew and place him into the carrier after the two ladies arrived. I thought of capturing MewMew myself at first, and while he was being petted it would be so easy, but I decided that they could do this better, since they had more experience in trapping cats, and thus perhaps I could avoid a scratch or two.

When Lori and the vet technician arrived, MewMew was out in the middle of the utility room floor. As they came into the room talking to each other, MewMew immediately recognized them. He jumped up what seemed to be 10 feet in the air and vanished from sight. I guessed that all the trauma of being neutered, sewed up afterwards, and especially the wound and the stitches, were still fresh in his mind. He must have recognized the two ladies' voices as well; I suppose he associated these unpleasant and painful experiences with them. Thus, in his attempt to escape, he found his way into the ceiling rafters. The two ladies were on a time schedule and could not stay to attempt to capture MewMew, which would have been futile in any event. So, I told them that I would bring MewMew to Lori's house as soon as I could capture him, and they could take care of removing the stitches there. I would then pick him up after this was accomplished. Little did I know then that it would not be that easy.

MewMew was so spooked by the sight and sound of the two ladies, that he was determined to remain in the rafters (The ceiling under the rafters is a large open area the entire width of the rec room. It is an open area of at least 25 by 15 feet). Since the area between the ceiling and the rafters is a narrow and completely open crawl space, there was no way anyone could reach inside and grab MewMew. The poor scared cat stayed in the rafters and would not come down. We placed fresh food and water daily on the floor of the utility room, just as before, but in a central area where MewMew was sure to see them, and hopefully smell them. I went on calling the cat to come down several times a day, but MewMew remained oblivious to our efforts to feed him. I heard him mewing every now and then, and even saw him coming close to the edge of the rafters' opening. I opened the small window in the window well of the utility room across from the edge of the rafters, and pulled back the curtains. I could see MewMew longingly looking at the window. He could hear the birds chirping outdoors. The sadness of not being out in the open and being trapped in the dark rafters, in spite of it being of his own doing, was evident in his big green eyes. I knew that he longed to be running and playing outdoors as he always did. However, days went by and the cat never came down to eat, drink, or use the litter box.

Soon I detected a slight whiff of a smell and determined that MewMew was probably peeing and pooping onto the ceiling under the rafters. I was becoming more and more alarmed with each passing day. I called Lori and she indicated that the cat was bound to eventually come down, and that he was not about to starve to death, but I was not so sure, and was beginning to wonder whether this would ever be. I called the Humane Society, but they could offer no advice. I even called the local Animal Control organization run by the County. They dispatched an officer who looked around my utility room and suggested that if nothing happened, the ceiling may eventually have to be torn down. In the meantime, he also suggested that I call an exterminating company that specialized in removing squirrels or other small animals from attics, to somehow force the cat out.

I contacted two companies who advertised that they removed wildlife from attics. One of them indicated that they only dealt with wildlife, such as raccoons, squirrels, birds, rodents, etc., but not with cats, and the other company said they could come out, but could not guarantee the removal of the cat without an injury, and that there would be a $300.00 nonrefundable charge for attempting to do so, even if they did not succeed. I declined, for after careful consideration I gathered that they probably could not accomplish this task, and I would have to pay them anyway.

On the fourth day I could no longer bear the thought of how miserable and hungry poor MewMew must be. The thought that by now he must be dehydrated, and that he may even die up there without some quick help, was becoming more real every day. After discussions with my son, I determined that I could possibly place a piece of plywood on the wire shelf which was located a few inches below the rafters. I could place food baited with tuna and the strong smell thereof would perhaps bring the cat out to start eating and drinking water, albeit on the shelf under the rafters, but within reach, after placing a step-up stool below. This chore was accomplished, and as we suspected, MewMew descended upon the shelf to eat and drink. Immediately thereafter he would disappear back into the rafters.

Now that the problem of the cat starving to death was resolved, there still remained the problem of MewMew's pooping and peeing onto the ceiling under the rafters, and our extreme anxiety of getting him out of our basement.

Three or four more days went by and the removal of the stitches was now about a week overdue. I had the idea of grabbing MewMew while he ate and placing him into the cat carrier that was outside the utility room door, so he would not catch a glimpse of it. When I discussed this with my son, we decided that this might not be easy due to the size and temperament of the cat, but would be worth a try. It would be better for my son to attempt to grab the cat, since my hands were weak, and he would be able to keep a stronger hold on MewMew than I would.

In order to facilitate this event, he would be bringing MewMew's food and water to him daily, for at least two or three days, before attempting to grab him, so that the cat could get used to his being there. We both realized that this might be our last and only chance of ever rescuing MewMew from the rafters.

Three days after my son started bringing MewMew's food and water, and on the fateful day that he would attempt to grab MewMew, he put out the cat's food and drink as usual. MewMew started to let out a slight growl as my son fed him, which he did not do when I fed him. After MewMew was eating for about two or three minutes, I called to my son from outside the open utility room door to start the capture. I felt my hands shaking. My son grabbed MewMew, but I did not see him do so. I only heard this horrible yelp which filled the house and practically caused the room to vibrate. Aaron then came out of the utility room carrying MewMew and placed him into the cat carrier, and we locked the carrier door. He said he had to squeeze MewMew pretty hard to keep him from escaping. He hoped that MewMew was not injured in the process, or had not damaged his claws, which he used to attach himself to the plywood, so that my son could not lift him.

Words cannot describe the elation and relief that we felt. I immediately called Lori's house but received no answer. I told my son we would go there anyway and drop the carrier off. We did this and placed the carrier on a metal chair next to her front door. Since it was dark, we felt that it would be safe for the cat and the carrier to be left there. Later that evening Lori called and indicated that the carrier should have been placed inside the back yard gate, for someone could have come by, let the cat out, and stolen the carrier. I felt like a ton of bricks was lifted off my back, knowing that the cat was out of the rafters and was receiving the care he needed. The next day I called Lori, and she noted that the stitches were removed, that the cat did not seem to be hurt, nor did his claws appear to be damaged. I must have been happier that day than at any previous time in my life, except perhaps on my wedding day.

After the stitches were removed, Lori kept MewMew at her cat house in our cat carrier, rather than letting him loose once again, while the flesh under the just-removed stitches had time to relax.

MEWMEW IS FREE AT LAST

That whole procedure, including the neutering, rabies shot, deworming, ear cleaning, flea treatment, general check-up, sewing up the wound, and the removal of stitches afterwards, cost very little. I could not believe how minimal the fee was, compared to what I was paying my vets for occasional visits by my two cats, and how lucky I was to have come across Lori of Metro Ferals, who was able to accomplish this feat.

We picked up MewMew the next evening and I placed the cat carrier onto our front stoop where MewMew had always come up to eat. There the food was already laid out for him, and we turned the carrier so that he would be facing the foil containing the food, and be able to smell it. When we opened the carrier door, he zipped out with great speed and vanished behind the building. I thought I would leave him alone to find his food, and he must have done so, because when I awoke later that night and looked out onto the front stoop, the foil was cleaned of the last crumb, as has always been the case, alerting me to the fact that it was probably MewMew and not some other animal who consumed it.

The next morning MewMew was at the front door when I opened it at 6:30 a.m., awaiting his morning feeding. Thereafter, he appeared at his usual feeding times twice a day, as if nothing had ever happened, and without missing a beat. A few days elapsed and he seemed to be more receptive to my attention. In addition to letting me pet him, he would butt his head on the back of my legs, and I noticed that unlike his previous habit of roaming the neighborhood, he was inclined to stick around the general perimeter of our building, or wander into the bushes across the alley from our house. When he walked on the small sidewalk around the building, he did not venture out of sight. He also seemed to enjoy sitting and lingering on the front steps, softly growling at passers-by walking their dogs, and generally enjoying the wonderful weather we were having at the time. When I called my two cats to come in before dark, he would also come running. I commented to my son that never again, as long as I lived, would I let MewMew into the house unrestrained in a cat carrier. MewMew began to occasionally climb onto our back deck through a small opening in the fence, and I nicknamed him "sentry." This was done after he determined to guard the front and back-deck entrances and keep out any and all intruders, including my own two cats.

When a strange grey kitty with a white neck resembling a bib appeared, I realized that it lived in our neighborhood. The kitty was very clean, as if just having had a bath and was wearing a collar. The kitty apparently sensed that there were other cats in the area and wanted to come around to socialize. However, MewMew was approaching it in a threatening fashion, growling softly. Sensing a fight, I shooed the pretty grey kitty away, and it never returned. On my walks through the neighborhood I ran into this kitty on a few occasions, and it mewed every time I approached, probably complaining of being lonely. It let me pet it, indicating that it was a tame kitty, living close by. Another beautiful kitty, white with grey spots, appeared across the alley from my house. It too wanted to socialize with our cats. However, my black cat Tiss saw it first and started growling. Tiss is very territorial. The white kitty was not deterred and shook its paw as if to say "Hi!" I knew that this kitty lived behind our building, for it had two tags on its collar – one tag containing its name and phone number and the other its address. Even though MewMew did not see this kitty, upon a very unwelcoming growl by my cat Tiss, it too never returned. Thus I felt that MewMew, along with my cat Tiss, would protect our home from any intruders be they cats, squirrels, possums, raccoons, or even people. After all, why would I need a security alarm system, when I had my sentry guarding the entry!

Most of the time when I opened the front door to either sit on the stoop, call my two cats in, pick up the mail or just head for the car, MewMew would come running to me wanting to be petted. These days when I sit on the step of the front stoop, he even crawls under my knees, but when I pet him in areas such as his stomach, he still tries to nip me with his claws. Otherwise, he likes to be talked to, and usually responds with a polite mew. He also likes to have his head and neck scratched and his back rubbed. What a ham!

As far as cats' names go, I prefer short and sweet names, such as Tiss, Toots and MewMew. On the other hand, my relative and her daughter like long, exotic names such as Babylonia (Babs for short), and Isadora (Izzy for short). They even honor their cats by mentioning their names on the voice mail, which is answered: "Betty, Ramona, Sherman and Gilbert are not available ..." Sherman is their deceased cat and Gilbert is their most senior cat. Since both these ladies are artists, it is not surprising that they can be so creative!

**TREATING MEWMEW'S FACIAL WOUND;
MEWMEW IS GIVEN A BATH**

One morning my son Aaron came in advising that it looked like MewMew was once again fighting. I ran outside and noticed that there was a small round facial wound dripping fluid, right above MewMew's eye. The area around the small wound looked as if it had been shaved. I immediately mixed a solution of water and peroxide, and with a paper towel dipped in, managed to rub the wound a couple of times while MewMew ate. Later I bought some first-aid antibiotic ointment and slapped it on the general area of the sore. I repeated these processes twice a day, and surprisingly MewMew let me do it.

To add insult to injury, as MewMew sat napping under the old oak tree in front of my stoop, a bird sent a large poop below, which landed on MewMew's back. The poor startled cat jumped up and started running around in circles for a few seconds, before disappearing into the bushes. Somehow MewMew related this incident to my being there. He avoided my presence, and would not let me approach nor pet him for the remainder of that day.

When a few days of cleansing and antibiotic treatment of the small facial wound did not produce improvement, and the infected area appeared enlarged with more of an infection setting in, I decided to once again visit the vet clinic. This time I was able to easily lift MewMew after his early morning meal, and carry him into the cat carrier which was located behind the front door. My son held the door open for me so that MewMew could be quickly placed into the carrier. MewMew was mewing a loud objection, but seemed to quickly settle down.

I called Metro Ferals to request Lori to take MewMew to her vet clinic, but was unable to reach her. Since I knew the name and address of the clinic, however, I made arrangements for a friend to take me there. As my car was not functional at the time, and since the clinic's location was in the city, in a neighborhood which was quite a distance removed from where I lived, and a neighborhood with which I was totally unfamiliar, I was happy to have a friend take me, especially since she got directions from the internet. Luckily she brought another person with her to further assist in locating the clinic. We spent about an hour driving around in circles in the intense 90-degree plus heat in a car without air conditioning, before we ever got there. Luckily there was no appointment needed, and there were only a couple of people there (the remainder of the customers having dropped off their pets for treatment).

The vet had to sedate MewMew in order to examine him. He gave MewMew a strong antibiotic shot and gave me some antibiotic ointment to apply to the wound twice daily. The vet technician advised that if the wound did not heal, I was to try another ointment, a ring-worm ointment, which she also provided to me, and indicated that one or the other plus the shot should do the trick. The vet technician stated that this condition was not serious, and there was no need for concern. In spite of the long and hectic trip, I was happy that I went to that clinic. I had a special confidence in this particular vet, who treated many feral cats and thus had experience with this type of cat.

When MewMew came home I brought the cat carrier indoors and set it by the air conditioning vent. About an hour or so later, MewMew came out of sedation and started to mew. I did not let him out into the intense heat, but after the sun set and it cooled down a little, MewMew was back to normal. I took the carrier outside and let him out. He was so happy to run out of the carrier, and started rolling on the grass! Sure enough, after about a week of antibiotic ointment application, and the shot, MewMew's face was totally healed. I was told that he might not have gotten into a fight, but merely acquired a skin infection that caused the wound and the bald area to appear.

I very much regretted that I failed at the time to ask the vet to arrange for a bath for MewMew, since he could really use one. When I would pet him, instead of the thick, soft fur, I would feel the dirty, matted fur. His fur has an unpleasant odor. MewMew desperately needed a bath and especially a flea and tick treatment since the fleas and ticks were a constant worry to him. Lately he had been scratching a lot, and even more worrisome, was that his whole body shuddered every so often, probably from the tick and flea bites. He occasionally mewed pitifully, and then said "bhk, bhk," which I interpreted as "It's miserably hot, and the bugs are biting!" I called the vet technician and found out that MewMew would have to be sedated in order to receive a bath and a flea and tick treatment.

On the day the vet technician suggested we come in, MewMew and I traveled to the city. This time, however, I found a shortcut to the clinic and went by myself.

Going back and out of the city there was not as much traffic as coming in in the morning. When we finally got home after what seemed to have been a process of several hours, since we had to wait for MewMew to be bathed and treated, I brought the cat carrier into the house, and placed it by the air vent for cooling comfort. Several hours later, when MewMew had totally recovered from sedation, I took him outdoors and let him go. He immediately ran into the bushes. Soon after he came out, looking so good and clean, and wanting to be petted. I was so proud seeing how handsome he had become, and the cat that he now was as compared to the cat I first met, seemingly so long ago. I could not resist planting a smooch onto his head. He responded immediately by letting out a loud sneeze! Poor MewMew, he just did not understand the magic of that first kiss.

WILL MEWMEW LIVE OUT HIS LIFE IN THE ALLEY, HOPEFULLY AS A HAPPY AND HEALTHY CAT?

Is MewMew a different cat today from the cat we first met so long ago? I would say so. MewMew is a lot more mellow. He is even more tolerant of visiting cats.

When Palusa, the cat who lives across the street first came over, I looked at her tag which had her name and phone number. She is a beautiful black, long haired cat with a big fluffy tail, large green eyes, and is certainly the tamest and friendliest cat I ever met. She immediately started to rub against my legs, rolled over on her back, and lifted her paws, as if asking for a stomach rub; she then proceeded to my door and wanted to enter the house! After taking it all in, MewMew merely swiped her once with his paw, to which Palusa responded likewise. Although much smaller and frail in appearance, she did not hesitate to face MewMew and was even prepared to fight him if need be (which luckily did not happen). I was surprised to see that when Palusa tried to eat MewMew's food and drink his water, MewMew just looked at her as if to say, "What are you doing?" and did not stalk nor charge her as he would have done previously to his being neutered.

Poor Palusa, when she first came over I had to feed her in spite of my son's warning not to do so. She was very hungry. I called the phone number on her tag and found that it was not a good number. I immediately tried to get her adopted out. I called the Humane Society but they could not accept any more cats at that time; they sent me a list with rescue groups' names and addresses. I found only one that would accept Palusa. It was a group called "King Street Cats." I made arrangements to drop her off early the following week. The next day Palusa showed up on my stoop, and once again, attempted to eat MewMew's food. A few minutes later, a child on a bicycle came by and said, "I know where this kitty lives." I asked her to show me and she walked with me across the street, past a few houses to Palusa's home. The lady who opened the door spoke little English. However, her daughter was able to translate and said that Palusa's vet ordered her to be on a diet. I remarked that she was quite frail and did not seem to need a diet. I asked them to feed her before letting her out of the house so that she would not eat MewMew's food. I immediately called King Street Cats and advised them that we found Palusa's home.

Since the townhouses where we live are so close together, and are actually attached to each other, I was concerned about three black cats lingering on my front stoop and porch, afraid of what the neighbors would say. The neighbors may decide to call the Animal Control, complaining that the place was overrun with cats, when in fact there were usually only two cats outside the house (MewMew and Tiss. Toots never lingers outdoors, but disappears as soon as she comes out). Fortunately Palusa does not stay long, and so what choice do I have but to put up with her at the present time.

As for MewMew's health and happiness, he has gained quite a bit of weight and I was worried of its effect on his health. The vet did not seem to mind, however, and I was told by a friend that the extra fat is a source of insulation for him during the cold winter months. He now has had all of his shots and even had his teeth cleaned.

When my son comes home from work, MewMew runs up to him and greets him. MewMew looks good and seems to feel good. He runs around, forever paying attention to everyone and everything going on in his territory. He still cannot enter my house, nor does he wish to do so, but in his outdoor domain he is the king of all animals and all things nonhuman. He knows that he is loved.

METRO FERALS' AND LORI'S DEDICATION; GENERAL COMMENTS

In an interview, Lori of Metro Ferals, discussed the problems encountered with the work that she has been doing for the last 10 years. Alley Cat Allies refers all local calls to Metro Ferals. People would then need to come in and pick up a trap, and trap the cat(s) in order that they may be spayed, neutered, receive the required shots and be checked for any diseases. Remembering that spay/neuter not only reduces the population of unwanted litters, but also reduces disease, bad smells associated with unaltered males who run after female cats, fight, and sometimes get injured, as has been the case with MewMew.

At one point Lori became aware of 10 to 15 cats residing under the loading dock in the public works facility in Washington, D.C. She trapped them and spent a large sum of her own money to have them spayed and neutered. Another time she conducted a rabies quarantine for 17 feral and 10 tame cats. Some of these cats were going to be transported to horse farms. Lori advised that farms are good for feral cats. The cats keep diseased predators out and alleviate the nuisance of rodents.

In addition to providing a house where 60 feral cats dwell at the present time, Lori also builds and sells at cost, and sometimes provides free of charge to those in need, plywood insulated shelters which are similar to a dog house, but somewhat smaller, for the use of caretakers of ferals. I am still amazed at how beautiful some of the cats living in her cat house are.

When asked what is urgently needed by her organization (other than funds, of course), she said that there is a shortage of volunteers who could provide foster homes for kittens that can be tamed, and ultimately adopted into good homes.

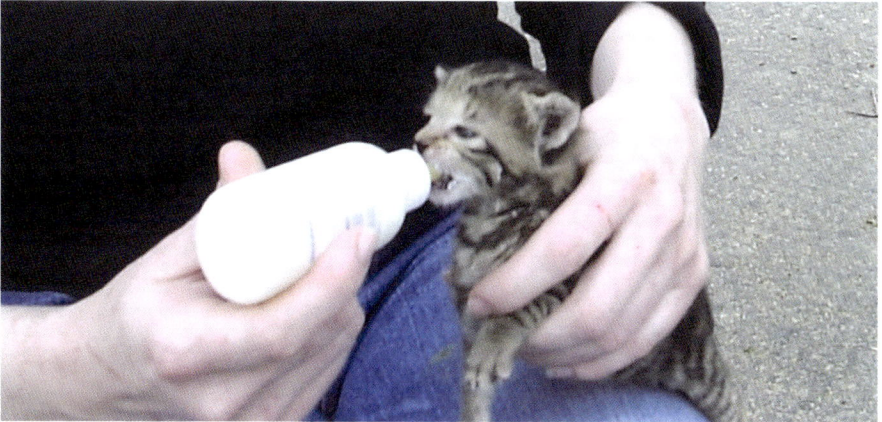

An orphan kitty being fed by an associate of Metro Ferals

Lori personally visits Washington, D.C. neighborhoods when she receives calls of feral cats in need of help. She attempts to trap and collect as many of them as she can, providing information and assistance to people who want to become caretakers of feral cats. She also provides information and allays complaints regarding the so-called environmental destruction and disability concerns.

Lori indicated that one of the big problems facing homeless cats in general is that there are just not enough homes for them, so millions of homeless cats languish in shelters around the country and are ultimately "humanely put down." In the opinion of feral cat and animal activist organizations, as well as many individuals, there is really nothing humane about euthanizing a healthy animal. It is vital therefore to spay or neuter your pet in order to minimize unwanted litters. You can receive information on this service by accessing the web site of Alley Cat Allies at www.alleycat.org.

It is also important to remember that should you want to acquire a pet, it is best to go to your community shelter, the Humane Society, or a rescue group, holding a public adoption.

Recently we purchased a cat collar and tag with MewMew's name and our phone number engraved thereon, in order for him to have a minimal measure of security, in the event of some unforeseen occurrence. We are still attempting to find just the right minute to grab him in order to affix the collar, which is proving to be a little difficult. It pays to take precautions, however, as one never knows what the future holds.

I now leave you with a thought that kindness to animals makes a better world for all of us -- meaning that people and animals need to live in harmony with the earth as one.

PHOTO GALLERY

MewMew is on the prowl

MewMew is considering his next move

41

MewMew is enjoying the last rays of daylight

*This morning MewMew received a bath,
and is now awaiting his supper*

At twilight MewMew relaxes after supper

MewMew is on the way to being a healthy and happy cat

The End.

1509960

Made in the USA